FROM THE ELUSIVE MUSE'S LEXICON

GARRY B GROVE

All rights reserved
Copyright © Garry B. Grove, 2020

The right of Garry B. Grove to be identified as the author of this
work has been asserted in accordance with Section 78
of the Copyright, Designs and Patents Act 1988

The book cover is copyright to Garry B. Grove

This book is published by
Grosvenor House Publishing Ltd
Link House
140 The Broadway, Tolworth, Surrey, KT6 7HT.
www.grosvenorhousepublishing.co.uk

This book is sold subject to the conditions that it shall not, by way of
trade or otherwise, be lent, resold, hired out or otherwise circulated
without the author's or publisher's prior consent in any form of binding or
cover other than that in which it is published and
without a similar condition including this condition being imposed
on the subsequent purchaser.

A CIP record for this book
is available from the British Library

ISBN 978-1-83975-416-6

FROM THE ELUSIVE MUSE'S LEXICON

Poetry Volume Two

Garry B Grove

"Truth is subject to no prescription, for truth is truth though never so old, and time cannot make that false which was once true."

Edward De Vere 1550 - 1604

Contents

A Glint of the Spectrum (In Perspective)	1
Collective Spirits of this Great Universe	2
Fate and Fortune of the Flowing Thames – Under London Skies	3
River	6
Sounds of the Rolling Sea	7
War on Your Doorstep	8
The Season of Uncertainty	9
Ghost in Her Wedding Gown	10
Ancient Citadel in Flames	12
Mystery Plays (1392-1579)	13
Godgifu, Woman in the World	14
Her Name It Is Eugenia May	15
Into the World of O'Carolan	16
Paean to a Departed Celtic Troubadour	18
High Above Chesil Beach	19
Beneath the Pagan Moon	20
In Search of the Elusive Muse's Lexicon	21
A Trial of Some Torturous Madness	22
Reveal Yourself to Me	23
In Fairest Florence and Tuscany	24
Made Our Way to the Eternal City	25
Venezia	26
Behind the Elizabethan Masque of Mystery	27
Broken Amphorae	29
Old Redwood Tree	30
Acer Tree	31

FROM THE ELUSIVE MUSE'S LEXICON

Four Seasons of Summer's Day Magic	32
Fragrant Wildflower Meadow	33
Green Avenues	34
On the Banks of Green Willow	36
Ode to a Passing Youth	37
Under the Deep, Blue Skies of Evening	39
Eve of a Crimson Moon	40
Midnight Encounter	41
Poem in the Present Tense	42
My Lonesome Escape	43
The Tenure of Childhood	44
Any Road up to the Summit (the Ruthless Pursuit of Power)	45
Ruthless State	46
All Power Diminishes	47
The Road to Ruin	48
To the Lighthouse	51
Words of the Fisherman	52
Upon the Green and Golden Hill	53
By Their Own Hand	54
Brittle Days	55
Some Burning Epiphany	56
Many and Varied Shades of Blue	57
Winter Days In To Reborn Spring Will Slip	58
We Two, This is Us	59
Along Cathiron Lane, New Year's Eve (2017)	61
Tree of Gold and Universal Dust	62
From Whence Came the First Origins of Man?	63
A Slice of Celestial Pie	64
For Absent Friends	65

This One is For J.B	66
When the Rules Get Burned (the Death of Democracy)	68
At the News of a Death	69
One Wish for a Winsome Child	70
Something for Posterity	71
The End – What's in a Title?	72
Dedications	73

Introduction

A Glint of the Spectrum (in Perspective)

A glint of the prism spectrum, schism in light of creation,
An encapsulated eminence of enchanted wonderment
Leaves me feeling like a sybarite reeling in awestruck admiration,
A crystalline refraction spills colours into the imagination,
In rapid rotation spins triangulation from modern to ancient,
A fracture opens within the psyche, time and space meet displacement,
Vermillion fire then indigo greet a trillion mists of ochre,
Broken emerald splinters linger, burning amber cinders enter
A million trysts of amethyst to golden centre, shades of blue
Sapphire breaking through, lapis, flint sparks, magenta
Brought into vision by a wondrous sensation, a trick of the light,
Observation of the axis centrum, a glint of the spectrum...

Forged from light and darkness to bring colour to these words.

Collective Spirits of This Great Universe

We may dance, we may sing,
Eulogise or curse,
In a trance, joys we bring,
In trouble or worse,
We are each one and all of us
Collective spirits of this great universe.
Faith, creed, basic need,
Philosophical differences,
Similar roads to traverse,
In doubt or indeed
With origins diverse,
We all breathe the same air
In the values we disperse,
We all share the same care
In discourse we converse,
We are each one and all of us
Collective spirits of this great universe.

Where we stand, what we think,
Proselytize or nurse,
Underhand, on the brink,
In clover or terse,
We are each one and all of us
Collective spirits of this great universe.
Many races on the same run,
Religious differences,
Similar roads to traverse,
In darkness or under sun
With disciplines diverse,
We all breathe the same air
With a deal in common,
For better or worse
In the hopes we summon,
Fast forward or in reverse
We all share the same care,
We are each one and all of us,
Collective spirits of this great universe.

Fate and Fortune of the Flowing Thames
– Under London Skies

When we ponder fate and fortunes of the flowing Thames,
London's stained and fabled, silver river,
From which it's city life stems.
Its comings and goings throughout history,
Life taker, life giver, a careworn Crown of Thorns,
Old John Barleycorn, mix of drink and religion,
Triumph and scorn, knowledge and power drawn
Along it's arterial banks to wither and thrive
In unity and division, derided and forgiven
Under London skies, to deliver new born and survive
Great fire and scourge of plague upon its people,
Dark the night, bright the spark of fire in their hands,
Where London stands, overlooks its antiquity,
Courage and desires realised in days illuminated
Beside fate and fortunes of the sweet flowing Thames,
Deep and diverse, as it flows to the open sea.

London's famed and much tormented waters
Through which it's city life flows everywhere
Along an ancient thoroughfare it stems,
Carrying secret stratagems, sons and daughters
Under the highs and shadows of London skies,
Make their way across time and river air,
To fight the good fight, close to the eternal flame
Though dark the night upon the old Thames,
Still bright the vital spark of fire in their hands,
In the shadow of St. Paul's where it rises and falls,
Greets and beats a rhythm against its embankments,
Gladstone and Disraeli, the Old Bill and Old Bailey
Echo in its history, shape and fashion its story,
Great Temple of modernity, the citadel ornaments
A spiritual source of liquid life,
This tour de force flows on ceaselessly.

FROM THE ELUSIVE MUSE'S LEXICON

In the Globe and Rose there Shake-Speare sounded,
Where Milton and Blake did first awake.
Here Boswell listened as Johnson expounded,
Where Dickens walked the dark streets of his prose
In this city that never sleeps, of Marlowe
And of Samuel Pepys, heaven knows
Their legacy into its very fabric seeps,
Where the distant past and future meets
As the sacred river flows, contains
London's pulse, its heart and veins,
Yet the ancient river rolls on to make
Its way with great momentum, the quantum
And invention, under lows and highs of London skies
Within its people's daily joyfulness and strife,
To crystallize the hopes and dreams that rise
Along its winding course through London life.

Soiled and sacred, the ancient silver river flows on
Through World order and hourly spontaneity,
Through the sorrow and the gaiety that pays homage
To the blessed river deity, its mystery and glory
Shaped the City's long, eventful history,
As savvy and gaily, today's crowds mill and mingle
Past Parliament Square with an occasional
Air and singular debates which rage on daily,
The old river runs freely toward the Tower,
World War Two "Blitzed", pounded, hounded its flower,
But still the City and the river they run freely
Toward the time and hour of growing
Financial power, when money talks loudly,
Peals its heavy bells and jangles loosely
To devour and heal, damage and blame,
To praise and shame its busy citizens.

Bridges of London brought forth growth and foundation,
Gave material lifeblood to commerce and wealth,
London's trading docks, its stocks and shares
Absorbed the shocks, through changing years
Of stealth and conformity, status and riches
Side by side with poverty, then came railways
Over and underground, brimstone and thunder
Station to station, the age of coal, iron and steel
Threaded, weaved its web of wires across the Nation,
Across the world, a dubious Empire built in fires
Of audacity and damnation, celestial diadems
Forged and banked in the name of salvation,
While the Bridges of London, Waterloo,
Westminster and Putney, as British as brown bread
Cheddar cheese and chutney, bonded its toughness,
Growing enormity, Tower Bridge, Hammersmith,
A whiff of tea and sympathy, Blackfriars, Lambeth,
Of late the Millennium, they all grace the river tides
Of venerable Londinium.

Within these dark and golden environs,
Journey there the frantic London denizens,
Between a chorus of sirens and Cathedral choirs,
Making fame and fortune, the name of the game
Pedantically played beside the glowing power
Of the vital, ever moving, fast flowing Thames,
From which omnipresent London City life stems,
Into the future paths and corridors of tomorrow,
While carrying echoes and voices of the past
Upon the ripples and resonance of water flow
Toward the ever changing ocean vast,
To come and go from source to estuary mouth,
Sweet Thames springs forth, shapes its course,
Ancient road diagrams strode over by pilgrims,
By horse, machines, crossed through time
Where the river sang, as it's lifeblood pours
Sweet Thames flows softly, Sweet Thames flows strong,
Londoners along its old banks do throng,
Sweet Thames flows softly, Sweet Thames flows long,
Under London skies it's spirit soars.

River

The river rolls on, the river remains,
The river flows on, through the landscape,
Through the veins,
Beneath warmth of the sun
Below cool moon and frozen plains
The river rolls on, the river sustains.

Water of life, of mystery,
Ever present fluid essence
Carves a path through centuries,
From its source springs constancy,
Flowing spiritual presence
Surges forth unto the sea
Clear and pure in efficacy
The river travels, the river explains
Power and strength of sanctity,
The river reveals, the river contains,
Winds its way through eternity,
Giver of life, of divinity,
Flowing spiritual presence
How its voice sings constantly,
Carves a path through centuries
Ever present, true quintessence,
Water of life, of mystery.

The river rolls on, the river redeems,
The river flows on, through the heartache,
Through our dreams,
Beneath quicksilver skies,
Below dark clouds and golden beams,
The river rolls on, the river serene.

Sounds of the Rolling Sea

Sometimes the sound of the rolling sea
and it's wistful waves
seem graceful, calm in melancholy,
But then the brutal tides
provides no one with the quality
of mercy,
Guides periled souls without restraint
to a reckless place of catastrophe,
Beneath rude surfs of the roaring sea.

When the tiny cockleshell priestess
plays her peaceful litany
and the air is filled with sounds of the
rolling sea,
Then sands will spill in hours and space
of a shoreline symphony,
A summer place of rest and haste
beside blithe sounds of the rolling sea.

When the young rock pool prince does
evince an air of reverie
and the sky is filled with sounds of the
rolling sea,
Then waters fill the strolling thrill along
a seashore of infancy,
Another time of golden chimes
beside the sounds of the rolling sea.

Other times, the pound of the roaring sea
and it's harmful waves
seem dreadful, storms of ferocity,
But then the sound of gentle tides
subsides for all with the jollity
of whimsy,
Guides absorbed souls with much to relate
to a peaceful place of great euphony,
Before the sounds of the rolling sea.

War on Your Doorstep

If you open up a window
And take a look outside,
There's a war upon your doorstep
From which you cannot hide.
Not the damaged who linger
For a small sample of grace,
Long after all the rhetoric
That disappears without trace.
Not the fearless who step forward
To represent the silent few,
But deep within the multitude
Well hidden from our view.
If you stand inside your doorway
And the blue horizon is wide,
There's a war upon your doorstep
That forms another divide.
Not the wounded who suffer
In some distant camera frame,
But in close, touching distance
Between the letters of your name.
Not those refugees who hunger
In some far-off barren space,
But right before your mind's eye
In the shadow of your face.
It may not appear too obvious
In a fleeting, casual glance,
There's a war upon your doorstep
That grants no second chance.
The perpetual conflict rages,
Day by day and year upon year,
Inside our newspaper pages
To sustain a quiet state of fear.
It happens without warning
At the break of every day,
Inevitable as a new morning
And it seems it's here to stay.
It's the people we are tomorrow
And all we think and say,
This war upon our doorstep
Could be the words we speak today,
This conflict on the doorstep
Burning in the light of day.

The Season of Uncertainty

When faith is low and nothing grows
But politics of misery,
Anger explodes in virtual prose
As rage is running globally,
Heaven knows in a golden glow
Direction chose instinctively,
People flow into the streets
In wild pursuit of liberty,
Pure hope meets to defeat
Regimes that speak of anarchy,
Holds overturned, bridges burned
Barricades broken, dogs run free,
Blind panic and profanity
Unleashes the season of uncertainty.

The season of uncertainty
A time when change is coming,
The season of uncertainty
Who knows the beat that is drumming?

Advertising signs on fire,
Brands and birth right here expire,
Smoke and flames, names are taken,
Icons token, harsh words spoken,
Everything is upside down,
Rebels block the roads to town,
Gunfire stutters relentlessly,
Power imposed ruthlessly
To quell the freedom surge,
To purge a questing urge
Of people living desperately,
To protect a house of infamy
Corruption stifles humanity,
This is the season of uncertainty.

Ghost in Her Wedding Gown

She appeared there,
A Ghost in her Wedding Gown,
In darkest of night,
In old Portadown,
Her beauty yet undiminished,
A handsome lover,
He went off to find the war,
Never returned
Through her open door,
So her life became unfinished.

In finest of white
She walked the chapel path,
Never to marry,
A tragic aftermath,
She took her life of lonely worry
To a place beyond
An early epitaph.

Faded rose petals
Covered the cold crypt floor,
Glory just a myth
In ravages of war,
Love destined never to return,
So her silent ghost
Still wanders in the loss,
Constant loneliness,
The dust and the dross,
His distant face in the after burn.

So many wasted young lives
Lost in wars and conflict,
Hearts that struggle to survive
Broken and derelict,
Love that harbours comfort,
Lives that witness pain,
Generations sacrificed
Again and again.
Upon the Russian steppes,
In Napoleonic battle,
In the trenches of Flanders
Bones and weapons rattle,
Man never learns from war,
Carnage and death tarnish,
No one keeps the score
For the millions that perish.
In the heat of raging war
Swords and sabres may flash,
Cannons will blast and roar,
Bury in chaos and trash,
Relentless is the noise,
No glory boys these
Innocents or Dogs of War
Careless death will seize.

She wandered there,
A Ghost in her Wedding Gown,
In darkest of night
In old Portadown,
Her lover's sweetheart now long stilled,
He went off to meet with fate,
Never returned
Beneath Menim Gate,
Their young lives remain unfulfilled.

In finest of white
She walks the churchyard path,
Between gravestones
And a shadow of the cross,
Never to marry,
Only to tarry in her loss.

Ancient Citadel in Flames

She stood upon a grassy knoll beside the trees
Observing an ancient Citadel in flames
In the near distance, a bright, fearsome glow,
Unmistakeable evidence of callous war,
Death and destruction in full force,
Buildings collapsing, Cathedral spire burning,
Medieval structures having stood for centuries
Broken, ravaged, scorched, blitzed,
An ecumenical history beyond a millennium
Wasted, devastated, ragged shadows of ruins
Immersed in fire and smoke, crumbling,
Falling, razed to the holy ground.

On a cold night in November 1940,
She stood upon a grassy knoll beside the trees,
From the relative sanctuary of a calm,
Leafy Kenilworth, a fourteen-year-old girl,
Watching what could be the world's end,
Not knowing who in her family had survived
Or perished, in searing heat of incendiary madness,
As if incessantly raining down, down, down,
Sparks of some satanic prophesy spiralling
Across urban skies, the shaking earth violated,
Naked spears of hatred shattering habitats,
Observing, helplessly, an ancient Citadel in flames.

Mystery Plays (1392 – 1579)

Within this ancient place on Holy ground,
Corpus Christi, Mystery Plays were once staged,
In bygone days, medieval pageants relayed
An anguished mothers' plaintive lullaby,
A heartfelt cry, at the plight of their younglings,
A profound lament, when Massacre of the Innocents,
Herod decreed to seek out the Christ child,
Bring mayhem to biblical Bethlehem's streets,
Force infant children to bleed, suffer and die,
To prevent the new Jerusalem, as Midsummer turned
Toward Christmastide, between dreaming spires
Of Cathedral and Holy Trinity, on hymn sheets
The Coventry Carol was made ready,
As people gathered before a choral serenity.

Now in these same ancient, narrow cobbled streets
Here in the modern-day city,
This earlier scene returns with ease,
Their resonance comes down to me,
Choral echoes through the centuries,
Along Hay Lane, Hill Top and Priory,
Into an open imagination…
"Bye, bye, lully"…comes down to me,
"Bye, bye, lully"…their heartfelt pleas,
Faith rituals held and spoken for centuries,
Mystical reveries, enter the conscience, speak to me,
In this present-day destination, the sensation of a link
Formed where Mystery Plays were once staged,
Down the ages to a choir boy's childhood memory.
"Bye, bye, lully"…returns to me.
"Bye, bye, lully"…their ancient pleas,
From a long bygone nativity,
Repeats in these hallowed streets again
Along Pepper, St.Mary's on Bayley Lane,
In the poignant Carol of Old Coventry.

(The Coventry Carol was broadcast by the BBC from the bombed-out St.Michael's Cathedral ruins at Christmas 1940, after the WWII Blitz upon the City took place a few weeks before on 14th November 1940).

Godgifu, Woman in the World

It is said Godgifu once rode, naked and majestically,
Astride her strong, white horse, through ancient, cobbled streets
Of an old, medieval Coventry,
To protest at levied taxes, more unwelcome adversity
By her husband, Earl Leofric of Mercia, bringing people
Even greater woes of poverty.
Time's candle burns and waxes, on such tales of uncertainty
Of old Anglo-Saxon folklore, when her flaxen hair alone
Created a curtain for her dignity,
Or was it merely an earlier tale of pagan mythology,
When fair Maid of May, in spring fertility rituals,
Stood before a sacred Cofa's Tree,
Long spoken upon pagan people's tongues, liberally
Down the distant, Middle Ages, to later draw the fabled
Lady Godiva story unto thee?
For the legend belied a truth behind the testimony
Of a munificent and powerful woman in the world,
Where males held full supremacy,
During the first half of a long, gone eleventh century,
Before a Norman invasion and Conqueror laid waste,
She made female power her legacy,
A figure such as an early Joan of Arc or a latter Boadicea.
Godgifu stayed strong, she retained her own lands,
Held respect in her hands of constancy.
So in her sense of fair play and duty, rode a naked beauty
With golden hair unfurled, along narrow City streets
Of an old, medieval Coventry,
A vision forbidden, was written into mythology,
When this woman in the world, gave refusal to defeat,
A bright beacon of woman's potency.
While tailor Tom was said struck blind for his indecency
When opening up closed window shutters before him,
A maelstrom then darkened his fantasy,
Countess of Mercia, gift of God by name and for clemency,
She stands tall in time's great hall of heroines,
Legendary within an old City's memory.

Her Name It Is Eugenia May

More radiant beauty possesses she
Than new light of dawning day,
Her name it is Eugenia, Eugenia May.
All the Seas and Sardinia,
Islands half a world away,
In tempo of an adagio,
More than silk or damask's sway,
She is rare;
No fairer luminescent
Than sublime Miss Eugenia May,

In the starlit clime above us
Where Gods and the Muses play,
Shapes substance of inspiration
Such as dreams and visions portray,
The song is of Eugenia, Eugenia May.

More loveliness adorns her energy
Than mere words we may convey,
Her name it is Eugenia, Eugenia May
A rose or fine gardenia,
Classic form of marble or clay
Forged by Michelangelo,
Impressions through the eyes of Monet,
She compares
To work of such eminence
Does divine Miss Eugenia May.

In the sunlit clime above us
Where doves and Angels stray,
Shapes substance and inspiration
Such as themes and legends relay,
This song is of Eugenia, Eugenia May.

Into the World of O'Carolan

You often spoke of O'Carolan
When you were but a wild, young man,
Then anger would soon find your lips,
Pure music in your fingertips
Would banish misfortune valiantly,
Along the way, the unknown journey,
Beyond mysterious barricades,
Across lost, deserted esplanades,
With equal mirth and melancholy
Upon the road and beside the sea,
A crucifix and a crucible,
Of broken dreams and whimsical
In the true Celtic tradition,
Through vagueness and precision,
You often played O'Carolan
In long and dark night's wintry span,
When you were but a wild, young man.

You entered the world of O'Carolan
When you were but a wild, young man
And this was how your yarn began.
Somewhat later than straight from the heart
After morning glories were torn apart,
We walked to the sacred river source
In fair or dark weather held our course,
Then danced along the winding bank
And best among our dreams did rank,
Where ripples failed to reach the shore
For just a while and for evermore,
A white dove crossed late afternoon,
A blackbird sang a song out of tune,
Behind folded emerald, sky unveiled,
There ghostly shades of sunset sailed
Beyond fallen arms of the undone,
Into open hearts of everyone.

Coolness chilled the evening air,
Hot summer became a long affair
For composition with paper chaste
Flights of fancy rolled and raced,
Up to the heights and down to ground,
Silence broken, released by sound,
Harmonic, symphonic, jigs and reels,
Music upped and took to its heels,
Beyond the river, over green fields,
Through a valley long concealed,
To less than golden city streets
Beholden to no one and discreet,
A Troubadour with songs galore
Rambled through an unknown score,
Blind harpist and a fiddler played
To leave Scheherazade in the shade,
When the world was well and truly made.

Paean to a Departed Celtic Troubadour

In this earthbound life we will not converse again,
Now your spirit has moved on
To inhabit old Tir Na Nog,
A state of melancholy settles upon me,
As flute, bodhran, fiddle and harp
Rescind into the Celtic fog,
One more incomplete entry written in pages,
Final stage exit made and played
Within a closed travel log.
A life's contribution should not meet with regret,
It was a joy to burn daylight with you,
And I am so glad that we two met
It was a pleasure to burn candlelight too,
For the hours that passed in the raise of a glass,
For moments we once shared and knew.
When the bluebells rise, within showers of rain,
At winter's demise, when complex is plain,
When simple is wise, in flowering of spring,
We may still hear your voice,
We may still feel you sing.
Your Celtic spirit will live long
In the hearts and minds of friends,
In the words of your mellow songs
To which there is no sorrowful end.
Let's hear it just once more, for the Celtic Troubadour.

High above Chesil Beach

Set upon a lone stile high above Chesil Beach,
Here distant horizons blend far from reach,
Where sun forms a glistening path across the sea,
This could be the waters of Galilee.

Silver and golden light reflects before the sands,
Free birds glide over wide salt sea strands,
Clear blue sky meets calm breeze across the sea,
This could be the waters of Galilee.

Olympian dreams being forged in the bay,
Human triumph and tragedy never far away,
No dark clouds to shroud the proud, open sea,
This could be the waters of Galilee.

Nothing here to come between you and I,
Beside green and golden hills and perfect sky,
Where sun forms a glistening path across the sea,
This could be the waters of Galilee.

Inside a vision of burning, natural colour,
Beyond bright summer glory and the dolour,
Between ripened harvest and withering tree,
This could be the green hill of Calvary.

Beneath the Pagan Moon

Broken coast walk fence
In shadow of the darkening sky,
You and I and a Pagan Moon
As a quickening world goes by.

No need for pretence
In the twinkling of a brightening eye,
You and I and a Pagan Moon
As we walk in the divine high.

A new day is dawning, another reason why,
Key to a gateway of renewed promise
Or a well that is running dry.
Sunrise greets the morning, another reason why,
Light in the doorway passing homage
Or a tumult that drowns a cry.

Daybreak over the ocean, we ask for no reply,
When the right chance is truly taken
Then the moment will not deny.
Sunset gives the warning, another day to defy,
Should the kindling spark be forsaken
Then the fire will surely die.

An unseen window opens
Into a burgeoning vista nigh,
You and I and a Pagan Moon
As the hastening time does fly.

We venture into the unknown
Surging through a burning Autumn sky,
You and I and a Pagan Moon
As a quickening world goes by.

In Search of the Elusive Muse's Lexicon

In light and shadows of mount Parnassus,
From Apollo's Temple to the Parthenon,
A lifetime's dreams they emerge and surpass us
In seeking the Elusive Muse's Lexicon.

Along Arcadian pathways we travel
Beside beings both joyful and woebegone,
Foreboding roads there before us unravel,
Revealing the Elusive Muse's Lexicon.

Pandora's Box of strange elements is open,
Seraphs and spirits here they all commune as one,
Voices in tongues of a language unspoken,
Unleashing the Elusive Muse's Lexicon.

An empty page or a life yet unwritten,
A journey through an age between here and gone
Under Sun and Moon and star bound, all smitten,
Unlocking the Elusive Muse's Lexicon.

She shows then leaves in silent evanescence
To find her centre of spiritual essence,
Down sacred aisles, such secret wiles,
She will astound by her physical presence,
In all my trials, my sweet denials,
Will I witness virtue's paragon?
Venture into the dark Priestess's Mansion,
Hidden locus where heavenly dust falls upon
To then visit with this literal pantheon,
Entering the Elusive Muse's Lexicon.

A Trial of Some Torturous Madness

Midnight blue,
The silken hue splendour of mystical night
Brings visions of your tender beauty,
Softly within my sight,
Upon broken wings rides forbidden promise
Foreshadowing sensibilities of wrong and right,
And as the full moon rages,
I turn empty pages of sheer loneliness
And longing without you in the night.

At the threshold of sleep,
At the instant of waking,
This love is as deep as a dream in the making,
At the sight of your smile,
At the merest hint of sadness
This love is a trial of torturous madness.

So I seek the warmth of your precious love,
While our short lives balance in precarious space,
I hunger for time to halt in our presence,
I linger for more than a fleeting embrace,
If we drift apart and our love it should perish
Then the moments we shared will remain in my soul,
In my head and heart I will silently cherish
When we reached for each other in the need to be whole.

As a child I saw the promised land,
In the stars, in the seasons, in the palm of my hand
And I tasted its nectar at the fountainhead,
But at this moment your love means more to me
Than anything I have ever done, or thought,
Or have said.

Reveal Yourself to Me

Reveal yourself to me
Before light is overcast,
The person you can be
When dreams are free at last,
When a door is open to see
An illuminated room,
Unchained from the dark past,
Liberty may then resume,
A branch of an olive tree,
A crystal flake of your soul
Just waiting there to unfold,
Reveal yourself to me.

Reveal yourself to me
Nebulous night will be done,
The person you can be
When future has just begun,
Take the universal key,
Breakthrough those cold defences
To meet the heat of the sun,
Discover hidden senses,
Unlock latent potency,
A crystal flake of your soul
Will burn in the stars like gold,
Reveal yourself to me
In words of poetry.

In Fairest Florence and Tuscany

Moving across this fine Renaissance landscape
Among cypress trees, citrus groves,
An Italianate sojourn, an escape
Under Florentine skies
Where amber wildness sunset roves,
In a state of grace realised.

We are blessed, music flows freely before us
In the form of a bright cadenza,
A sample of fleeting baroque sails by us
In the blissful City of Firenze.
It does arrest the senses, steals impetus,
A vision of archetypal splendour,
Candles burn in worshipful chorus
In celestial chapels of Firenze.

A mask of Dante's face at rest
Preserves the place of Divine Comedy,
We step over the Ponte Vecchio
A homage but no homily of adoration
After climbing the sublime Duomo
Of Santa Maria del Fiore,
A voyage but no odyssey surely
These few lines of declaration.
Moving across this fine Renaissance landscape
Among cypress trees, citrus groves,
An Italianate return, an escape
Under Florentine skies,
A wandering eye soon behoves
In a state of grace realised,
Veneration of antiquity,
Such beauty to attest
That of fairest Florence and Tuscany.

Made our Way to the Eternal City

Made our way to the Eternal City
Where temple lights never burn down too low,
Where steadfast, the spiritual beacon
Will not waiver or ever lose its glow.
When the dark downside greets a bright upside,
Slender existence is laid bare of thread,
Then those steady feet they will not falter
For those troubled feet they know where to tread.

Made our way to the Eternal City
Where brilliant truth never turns to dark,
Where the one metaphysical reason
Will not wander or ever lose its spark.
When a bright upside meets the dark downside,
Optimism will overcome the dread,
Then those weakened limbs will find shelter
And a strong heart will know which way to head.

Made our way to the Eternal City
Made a treaty with a love so divine,
Where a body of fleshly entity
With devotional essence may combine.
Between the sublime state and the pity
In a place where universal stars align,
Before the helpless souls and the witty
An ancient Pharos gives forth its sign,
And real sense of purpose will not alter
For the abandoned and the benign,
Then those steady feet will not falter
And those weakened limbs will find shelter,
On the road to hope and integrity
At the Gates of the Eternal City.

Venezia

Venezia,
Tired and overworked City of the sleepless lagoon,
A place of faded, serenaded,
Highly elegant eccentricity,
Born of mercantile magnetism,
Built on a tradition of maritime energy,
Fragile centre of fluid gravity,
Historic blend of high culture
And once clandestine depravity.
It's network of canals
Channel ancient trysts of romance
And star mapped mystery,
Remarkable artefact,
Relic of glorious antiquity,
Kingdom in the sea,
Inside the Salute inspires
An epiphany,
So beautiful, we just want to marvel
And gaze at thee,
Longingly, La Serenissima.

Venezia,
Lovers, wheelers and dealers, under the moon
Haunt its waterways from former centuries,
The Bridge of Sighs, the scene of sins,
A Masque conceals its sanctuary,
Disguises its venerable dignity
Of seafaring destiny and dolphins
In Islands of Venetian majesty.
Across your waters, music streams,
A sound scape of Renaissance dreams,
Sonic ripples stretching outwardly
Toward the Adriatic Sea,
Eternal tides that wash and rise
Over thee, skyline jewel,
Kingdom in the Sea, birthplace of Vivaldi,
It makes a silent fool of me,
I Silenzi Di Venezia

Behind the Elizabethan Masque of Mystery

For this tale is darkly written,
Codified and powerfully denied
By hidden forces, fearsome and driven
Beneath a thespian masque,
Finely wrought and riven,
A genius long effaced
In silent, heinous task,
Authorship then misplaced,
The literal truth is forbidden.
Fate has taken away choice
And time its chiming toll,
Art of Phoebus' stolen voice
Set in motion the rhyming roll,
Lit by language lucid and lyrical,
Secret discourse of the soul
Of tacit resources put to work,
Born of language loyal and mystical,
Wordsmith toiled to ignite a flame
Beneath the surface, a hidden practice,
Revelry never to be the same.
A courtly activist lit a spark
Sent burning through the ages
Measure for measure, mark for mark,
Spear-Shaker, hand on the pages,
Courage of youth, stolen fame,
Seeker of truth, a Tudor sage,
Blazing wonderment, never tame,
Edward Evergreen "Soul of the Age",
Another name set in the frame
In the quick of a darkening sky
Apollo is taken, identity mistaken,
By devious hands that deceive the eye.

FROM THE ELUSIVE MUSE'S LEXICON

Behind the masque of mystery,
Subterfuge, sleight of hand,
Erased a name in history,
Politics of poison, power abused
In familial treachery,
A stranger in his own land,
Poetry and plays misused
For fourfold of centuries.
Now the truth is rising
Through the golden lines,
A covert mask is lifting,
Peeling from a thin disguise,
An error to be rectified,
Truth will outweigh the lies
Of an author sanctified
In Westminster Abbey,
Beneath a false monument
A dark deed once shabby
Will spring into the light,
The flame will burn
In its rightful name,
True Shake-Speare emerging bright.

Broken Amphorae

Broken amphorae buried in time's
Accumulated universal debris,
Etruscan relics maybe, waiting on a shoreline,
Some place undiscovered,
Ancient artefacts hidden from human touch
For many centuries.

Vessels, once carriers of wine,
Humble possessions of a long, forgotten dynasty,
Emerging in the modern age,
Dormant in destiny, bypassing events
Of human history
For many centuries.

Revealed by the ceaseless tides
Of an unerring ocean,
Beneath cerulean skies and burning sun
In sand grains, bearing stains of aeons
And wave motion stirring
For many centuries.

Beside the Tyrrhenian Sea
Careworn artistry, encrusted over
Timeworn terra cotta, basking on a shoreline,
Shipwrecked cargo, lost
Ancient artefacts, hidden from human touch
For many centuries.

Old Redwood Tree

When summer came upon us in its mystery,
Children played freely all the sun dance day,
Near an Abbey almost tenfold of centuries
There welcome was warm but not to outstay,
A constant figure of natural harmony
Through passing years, joys and fears rolled away
Pain and pleasure in an equal measure,
Burned those hours of toil, rest and play,
Nothing would then come between you and me
Beneath cool shade of the old redwood tree.

When winter snows deeply mantled green scenery,
There a white blanket of purity lay,
Dearly held then was the prospect of liberty
Where a sweet garden of tall trees did sway,
A presence of ancient order and beauty
Through falling tears, bliss and cheer stilled the day,
Love and leisure in a trove of treasure,
Turned those hours that spoil, to repay
Comings and growing of our family
Beneath cool shade of the old redwood tree.

Acer Tree

In the garden, a beautiful Acer tree,
Speaks to the soul through its vibrancy,
Leaves the colour of Autumn burn,
Dappled light and pale shadows sway
Cast down by the warm sun's bright rays,
As a fragile Earth on its axis turns,
Releases spirit from weight of concerns,
When day is done
In the flow of humanity.

In the garden, a sea of tranquillity,
Roots and branches of nature's finery,
Unlike woodland of wild spring fern,
Nurtured by hand in man's way,
Sensory delight on display,
As all four seasons will pass and return,
Life's lessons they are lost unless we learn,
When day is done
In the flow of humanity.

Four Seasons of Summer's Day Magic

During an English summer's day
Four seasons may merge into one,
Where children do happily play
Beneath clouds and light of the sun.

Sunday church bells chime out and ring
Angels tread upon holy ground,
A day of rest takes to the wing
Gifts of goodwill are all around.

Happy birthday now May is here,
Blooming madly in full of spring,
Another year older I fear,
Flower strewn, fragrant meadows sing.

Allegro movement in the air,
Four seasons they merge into one,
Pastoral dance runs everywhere
Beneath clouds and warmth of the sun.

Joyously, among grass so green,
Spring and summer soon meet their match,
Children are all heard but not seen,
Festive schemes they dream and then hatch.

After an English summer's day,
Folk may feel that living is fine,
Fate, romance, not so far away,
No one left searching for a sign.

Four seasons in one summer's day
While working through this folio,
So please, do not blame me I say
Just blame it on Antonio.

Fragrant Wildflower Meadow

We walked in fragrant wildflower meadow,
Between sweet blooms and the scent of heather
At height of summer, beneath fair weather
Where sunlight cast its broken shadows,
Clear blue sky and dragonfly altogether
Beside the long and languid lakeside water,
Before a fragile house of cards fell in ruin
When the demon released his wayward daughter
And rain cascaded through an open vein
Upon frail foundations of much undoing,
Before pain invaded, like a knife to the brain,
To find a level of unbalanced silence brewing,
To see a trail of lambs led to their slaughter
With no vice or dark menaces to be left eschewing,
Beside the long and languid lakeside water
At sleight of summer, beneath fair weather
Where sunlight cast its troubled shadows
And hours passed to someplace forever,
As a new chapter collapsed untethered,
We walked in fragrant wildflower meadow.

Green Avenues

Down along old, leafy green Avenues,
Where formative years met with the Blues,
One's own story of Strawberry Field,
There did ripe imagination yield,
Sixties' summers of ideology
Through a changing times and biology,
Music came and fine words inspired,
Ignited dreams and minds became fired,
Golden flame burning those years of youth,
Everyone searching, three chords and the truth.
John Peel playing on the Radio,
One notch below Desolation Row
On a Sunday night in "The Wrinkled Teste",
A glass of Ale, Good Evening and Bless Thee!
A neglected Bandstand in Gosford Park,
Blue Afternoon then a smoke after dark,
In quaint, Edwardian elegance
Where you could take your rest or take a chance,
Step into your Red Shoes and dance in time,
Blaze a trail down the starry clime,
Maybe not so in the physical sense
But ipso facto, visions immense,
The past may haunt us, the past will define,
The story is yours, the story is mine,
A smiling phase were those purple haze days,
Early years spent navigating the maze,
Those Avenues were green then, as were we,
We all tried in our way to be free,
Above broken politics, terrorism,
Vast colours colliding through a prism,
Gaining momentum or losing control,
Music sustained, nurtured the soul.
Let It Be or just force it all to burn?
As questions arose, so leaves would turn
From green to gold but fast years do not wait,
Meet with the Temptress who will tempt your fate?
Stand inert at the Secret Garden Gate?
Offer Salome your head on a plate?
A head loaded with memories like these,
Down the sensory Avenue of trees,

Down along old, leafy green Avenues
Where formative years met with the Blues,
A clandestine liaison with the Muse,
Beginning a journey we each would choose,
Where golden leaves turn to burgundy,
Minds yearned for learning hastily,
The point of the compass span dizzily,
The story is you, the story is me.

On the Banks of Green Willow
(for George Butterworth)

A country dancer once ventured along
Sweet Shropshire meadows there laying fallow,
Over sweeping Sussex downs that resound
In search of traditional English folk song
Where purest dew drops fell to ground
And early mellow sunlight hid the gallows,
To meet soft echoes of lost pastoral sound
On the peaceful Banks of Green Willow.

Then he opted for a soldier's life,
A volunteer in the First World War
To grim killing fields of sacrifice
Like so many young men had gone before,
Where bravest blood drops fell to ground
A sniper's bullet wrote a final score
From dark shadows of death that surround,
Taken, as the first Somme battle did roar
Across the blood drenched trenches bound
To turn a wondrous life to ruinous gore.

A composer lost in nineteen sixteen,
Buried where he fell in soil shallow,
Yet still his music survives to astound
But his vibrant heartbeat will always belong
Where purest dew drops fall to ground,
A rhapsodic air his soul shall follow,
To greet soft echoes of pastoral sound found
On the wistful Banks of Green Willow.

Ode to a Passing Youth

Speak out you mind without restraint,
You drunken sinner, you mystical saint,
You gallant winner, you devious schemer,
You beautiful dreamer, you potentate,
Valiant crusader in the hands of fate.
Show me your pictures crystal clear,
You far away, you too damn near,
You star gazer, you secret believer,
You sweet deceiver, you matador,
Cap in hand beggar at providence's door.

Let me hear your soft-spoken voice,
You with great hope, you with no choice,
You wanderer of night, you wasted chance,
You fight the good fight, you crocodile tear,
You fumbling jester of yester year.
Save me from the sadness in your eyes,
You miracle worker, you thin disguise,
You constant habit, you figure of doom,
You shadow in the room, you star bright,
Partaker of the last and sacred rites.

Give me a sign of your true goodwill,
You quick city drifter, you Buffalo Bill,
You fast burner, you private person,
You head turner, you betraying kiss,
You see the message that others miss.
Show them you can pull right through,
You handsome joker, you moods of blue,
You all night smoker, you vital clue,
You owner of riches, you outstretched hand,
You stranger in this very strange land.

FROM THE ELUSIVE MUSE'S LEXICON

I feel you drifting away from me,
You gentle lamb, you cold misery,
You frail child, you wise old man,
You youth run wild, you hopeless faker,
You disenchanted life, you rain maker,
You victim of strife, you truth searcher,
You treasure seeker, you great pretender,
You trouble mender, you ritual dancer,
You helpless romancer, you Angel face,
You came so quickly and then left without trace.

Under the Deep, Blue Skies of Evening

Wending through the deep, blue skies of evening
As sundown slips away,
Electricity sparks at the edges of dark
As the daylight hours make way,
Lovers, weaving homeward while reasoning
At the quiet end of day.

Moving through the blue, blue skies revealing
As bright lights burn away,
Veracity glows where knowledge grows
As the starlight turns our way,
From distant constellations beaming
To reach this earthly sway.

Stepping beneath the blue, blue skies believing
As half-light grips the play,
Alchemy touches the outer reaches
Of a dark night in disarray,
Unsettles the order of the evening
As virtue of patience strays.

Walking under the deep, blue skies deceiving
As twilight dims the day,
Playmates procrastinate over their fate
As the daylight hours make way,
To banish any regrets remaining
At the silent end of day.

Blending in the blue, blue skies of evening
As moonlight shines away,
Felicity streams on the cusp of our dreams,
Shooting stars blaze and fade away
To leave a trail of moon dust gleaming
At the end of dark night's stay.

Eve of a Crimson Moon

Earth's shadow eclipses a blood red moon,
Beneath, random gypsies romance and swoon,
Dance in the half light of pagan night skies,
Advance, delirious across dark fields,
Radiance delights curious, wide eyes,
Gravity defied as lunar fire wields,
Glance amber crystal flakes upon the lake,
Forsake a jejune world, vibrant in wake,
Witness universal wonder in tune,
Earth's shadow eclipses a blood red moon.

Upon the eve of burning crimson moon,
Embers illuminate fate and fortune,
Dance in the half-light of pagan night skies,
Advance, mysterious through space untamed,
Brilliance ignites glorious, bright eyes,
Destiny written on planets un-named,
Chances untold, celestial flames ablaze,
Potency with a power to amaze,
Observe universal splendour impugn
Upon the eve of burning crimson moon.

Midnight Encounter

Midnight casts a dark conjuration
Across two figures seeking shelter,
In random encounter, disparus who
Meet on the edge, there is no cameo,
He is no Romeo, she speaks broken English,
Mouthing indiscreet language in shadow
By the jetty, her pallid beauty partly hidden.
He, an exiled St. Christopher approaches
Upon the dimly lit street corner,
A rambling sailor from rolling seas,
A harlequin chancer in a dance of mime,
A weary soldier from war torn skies
Looking to discover where his soul is.
He cannot believe she is for real,
A tumbled angel in a danger zone,
Medusa tempting his weaknesses,
Mary Magdalene to tend his wounds,
A strange, exotic creature
Or some misfit caricature,
In this cathartic liaison of lovers,
This cosmopolitan region of felicity.
Music streams around and about them
In smoke filled streets,
Carries across and through
Nuances of the night,
Captures their hungry hearts
Of passion and poison,
Stealing his rhythm,
Stealing her rhythm,
Carrying them both
Disarmed and defenceless
Into the esoteric midst
Of the evening masquerade.

Poem in the Present Tense

This life may be a long walk to oblivion,
A flickering journey through
A fast, burning flame,
To the centre of substance
Toward prominence,
A gilded gateway
Of fickle fortune and fame.
Hear then from real glories of innocents,
Listen to truthful stories of untold pain
From isolated spaces of pure sentiment,
While the damaged pay homage
To the profane.

When will the overdue human experience
Abandon the exclusive club and secret sect,
Break down outmoded barriers of ignorance
Give all peoples honest, dignity and respect?

Quotes from a libelled bible of idiom
When the compelling need for redemption calls,
Partake of a long pathway to oblivion
When that bleak, atoning hour of reckoning falls.

This life may be a long walk to oblivion,
A fleeting glance through the open window of time,
At the heartland of spiritual sustenance
To the Elysium of a power sublime.

See sorry shambles of tarnished excellence,
Look to officious chambers of dirty shame,
Erect stand pompous temples of indifference,
Where hollow hearts worship values of empty gain.

When will an overdue human experience
Abandon the exclusive cult and secret sect,
Break down outmoded barriers of sufferance,
Give all peoples honest, dignity and respect?

My Lonesome Escape

My lonesome escape,
To a shoreline where cool waves break,
Enticed into the beautiful light,
Found by an ocean of rhythmical sound
Beside the ethereal seascape.

Some quarrelsome state
In a desert of reason as landscape,
Invited into an inevitable fight
Bound by notions of reasonable ground,
Despite acts of a poisonous relate.
My wistful escape,
To a coastline where spirits awake,
Seduced by the most whimsical flight
Down to an ocean of mythical renown,
Along this magical seascape.

This troublesome fate
In the ruins of logic and heartbreak,
Ignited by a predictable blight
Crowned in a risible province of clowns
Like an invisible potentate,
Seduced by the most beautiful sight
Where the rueful evening sun goes slowly down
Upon my blue, lonesome escape.

The Tenure of Childhood

The tenure of childhood is not long, young one,
Though desire for adulthood is strong,
Bathe in innocence for yet awhile,
Wear new garments of spring in a smile
For the tenure of childhood is not long,
Time enough for the bittersweet song,
Good fortune rests within your own grasp
Through grains of sand and promised lands,
You have the power to break from the clasp
Luck's fault line travels between your hands,
The triumph of substance over style,
Candles will burn on the country mile,
Soon learned is treachery in the throng,
For the tenure of childhood is not long, young one,
To find balance between right and wrong
Through a journey of joys and trial,
For reasons you avoid and compile
To find a way forward and place to belong
For the tenure of childhood is not long.
From the first breath drawn to the last gasp
Weakness fails, positivity stands,
In comfort, ease or with burning rasp,
Blissful peace or the worst of demands,
Life is lost when spent in denial,
Drink from the draught of sweet youth's phial
So hold fast the infant glow to prolong,
For the tenure of childhood is not long, young one,
For the splendour of childhood is soon gone,
Bask in those moments before they are done
And the pathway to wisdom is long.

Any Road Up to the Summit (the Ruthless Pursuit of Power)

Any road up to the summit,
Any route to take us to the peak,
A game without any limit,
We'll make sure the future is bleak.
Any walk up to the summit,
Any soap that will gain us the seat,
We claim undeserved credit,
We make a victory of defeat.

Any mode that hands us the power,
Any road that secures us the throne,
We'll spin more angles each hour,
The monotone voice on your phone.
Any method that serves to control,
Any image that conjures the trick,
To capture the most critical role,
We keep communication slick.

Any road up to the summit,
Any track that will back up the cause,
Culture numbed as morals plummet,
The shoulders we stand on are yours.
Any path that reaches the top,
Any rhetoric to get to the goal,
Momentum that no one will stop,
We'll fix the price on your soul.

Any road up to the summit,
We can suspend disbelief,
We'll place your family in debit,
From this pain there is no relief.
Any poll to accomplish our aim,
Nothing can stand in our way,
We still arrive all the same.
Though we seldom do as we say.

Ruthless State

This place carries the odour of kerosene,
Speaks of ravage and obstruction,
Harbours suspicions,
The promise of pogroms,
No pleasantries exchanged here
In darkness abundant,
This place thrives on intimidation
On a grand scale never before seen.

This place indulges in acts obscene,
Cold and hard as granite
In desperate remedies,
Hires the bully boys,
Spectres of death and disease,
Makes compassion redundant,
This place threatens of ruination
On a grand scale never before seen.

This place empties contents of magazines,
Reeks of damage and destruction,
Burns down the missions,
Kills in the classrooms,
No dignitaries remain here
In cruelness abhorrent,
This place lives by recrimination
On a grand scale never before seen.

This place subjects all people to genocide…
A ruthless state, void of humanity,
Fuelled by hate, run by death squads,
This place builds its power and strength
In silent acceptance of its methods.

All Power Diminishes

As falling sand grains explain:
All power diminishes,
Through pleasure and through pain
Life essence ebbs and flows
Like dry sun, wild wind and rain
Burns, peaks and finishes,
All power diminishes.
Spent passion is never in vain
When purist intention replenishes,
Life essence ebbs and flows,
A spirit of merit burns on
And sustains
As all power diminishes.

Along crooked or straight lines,
In company of courage or fear,
The journey a character defines
Shaped and formed year by year,
As a circle unbroken repeats,
As the cycle of life revolves,
Where flesh and spirit meets
A pattern begins and resolves.

As sparking light guides the brain
A dark hour vanishes,
True measure of sacred refrain
Quintessence burns and glows,
Divine light shines and remains,
Love builds and cherishes,
All power diminishes,
Spent passion is never in vain
When brightest intention encourages,
Life essence dims and grows,
A spirit of merit burns on
And sustains
As all power diminishes.

The Road to Ruin

This hard journey there unfolds
Down a rough, perilous road,
Across dry, deserted ground,
A stark and hostile abode,
A dark road of undoing,
Down the bleak, precarious,
Deeply nefarious course,
The reckless road to ruin.
Where everything is lost,
All chattels you may own,
Along a harsh, friendless path
Where a soul travels alone,
Turns to face the aftermath
Down a dimly lit, crooked road
Through an empty lost and found
With neither value or code,
Dark web demons pursuing,
On the very dangerous force
The feckless road to ruin.

Lost souls wandering there,
Squandering precious time,
Void of purpose and reason,
No direction in careless ramble,
Gambling through shambles
Wasted in their prime,
As an inevitable fate
Awaits there coldly accruing,
Beyond the ever-open gate
To the tortuous trail of treason,
The delirious, heartless
State on the road to ruin.

Cognoscenti give counsel
In chaos and confusion,
Bold words of sage advice
Proffered liberally
In confident profusion,
Conventional wisdom's
Overworked solution,
To follow 'neath black raindrops,
In the grey cyber hollow
Shadows hover on the border,
Some cyclops minus vision
Uses true precision, screwing
With devices of disorder,
As discordant music stops
On the shallow road to ruin.

Blood is chilled to the marrow
Where fly the twisted arrows
Of outrageous fortune,
To impale the meek and narrow
With no escape from misfortune,
The gates are always closed
To those who know for certain
That uncertainty prevails
By the hour, then flowers
Seeds of failure in the gutter,
The clutter of misused power;
Legislators are busy suing,
The powerless who sail
Down the careless road to ruin.

FROM THE ELUSIVE MUSE'S LEXICON

Empty pockets picked relentlessly
In darkness without feeling,
Souls are stripped of dignity,
Overwhelmed senses reeling,
An hourglass without sand,
All is ambiguity,
All at sea with no dry land,
Absence of community,
Torture chambers close at hand,
No measure of impunity,
Austerity without plans,
No liberty, fraternity,
Nowhere with nothing doing,
Vanished for eternity,
Dreams implode on the crowded road to ruin.

To the Lighthouse

To the lighthouse
At the coastline,
Where evening stars ignite
Restless tide, waves reflected
In its beam burning bright,
To the lighthouse
At the shoreline,
We run with all our might,
We are guided, directed,
Through the darkest of night,
To the lighthouse
As the torch shines
Forming white streams of light,
Lost mariners connected
By deepest fears and plight,
To the lighthouse
A beacon shines
Relief within our sight,
Stands out boldly, respected,
Brings salvation despite
Perilous douse
And broken lines
In storming waters flight,
Ruthless cold, resurrected
Souls found in a blaze of light
By the lighthouse,
On a coastline,
Where evening stars ignite.

Words of the Fisherman

Did you heed the words of the Fisherman,
To have love and respect for fellow man,
To strive to be the best person you can?
Light in the darkness when night is cold and long
Voice of reason when doubt surrounds the throng,
When order breaks down and there is no plan,
Spite and blight reign across the Earth's span,
Do you heed the words of the Fisherman?

Do you hear the pleas of the Fisherman,
To deal in fairness with everyman,
For comprehending, a clear map to scan?
Hand of kindness when peace is hard to find,
Clarity when chaos engulfs the mind,
To live as a humanitarian,
Give equal weight to Bible and Koran,
Do you hear the pleas of the Fisherman?

For those are acts of kindness indeed,
Messages behind the code and creed,
Contemplation above condemnation,
Rumination above ruination,
Elevation above exploitation,
Did you heed the words of the Fisherman?
Did you carry the torch of the Fisherman?
Did you keep the watch of the Fisherman?
Did you walk the road of the Fisherman?
Did you sail the boat of the Fisherman?

Upon the Green and Golden Hill

Upon the green and golden hill, hidden from view,
There hidden still from the tiresome, tangled milieu,
Upon the green and golden hill, hidden from sight,
When life's fill of work is done and the time is right.
Good friends have now gone, friends have passed
Beyond pleasures of time that fade and will not last,
No final conversation, no considered last words
Inferred or spoken, patterns changed or broken
Before travelling into vast, inglorious night,
Way of all men, beasts and insects, flowers and birds.

Upon the green and golden hill, beneath the clouds,
Where dreams do spill, from seriousness disavowed,
Upon the green and golden hill, beside the trees,
The youth of eternal summers leaves with the breeze.

Upon the green and golden hill, above blue sea,
There an ocean spans out toward infinity,
Upon the green and golden hill, so far from reach,
Where toil is disregarded and time does beseech.
Good friends have departed, friends moved on,
Another epoch awaits for surviving ones,
Some brief contemplation, chosen lines of verse,
Not absurd or token, spirits calmed or shaken
Afore venturing into the blind and wild breech,
Time marks out each journey for praise or a curse.

By Their Own Hand

In the ethereal air we breathe
We remain to yearn and grieve,
When a life has suddenly departed
Leaving us but broken hearted,
Numbed in silence, overpowered,
When the seeds of death have flowered,
Taken from us with words unspoken,
Life force halted, a rhythm broken,
By their own hand so released,
We in our turmoil, they at peace,
In the ethereal air we breathe
We remain to yearn and grieve.

We believe we really know them,
All the love we chose to show them
Seems as nothing within a shadow,
Just a slight breeze through a meadow,
When the music stops to silence,
Mood and moment torn by violence,
Warmth and close presence has gone
Far the familiar one to one,
We take a full cup and lift it up
To ease our shattered dreams we sup,
All the acute pain would send us mad
To deal with the impossibly sad,
When the deeply troubled choose to leave
We are left to yearn and grieve.

Brittle Days

Brittle days, a spirit in free fall,
Everything seems to mean
Almost nothing at all.
Downward, dimming spiral, a world rushing by,
News going viral in the blink of an eye,
Vortex descending, in days that are so dark,
A life just held pending with no vital spark.
Brittle days, feelings left shattered,
Existence cold and numbed,
All senses battered,
There was a time
With a purpose that mattered.
Brittle days, a dream turned sour,
A clock hand has frozen
At a point in the hour,
An old church, a dusty bible
Tributes flow, saddled with grief
That has no place to go.
Brittle days, no relief,
Moments suspended in disbelief
A road less travelled, a lack of order,
Broken tokens strewn all along the border,
Empty gestures, flowers and fauna,
At some point in the distance
We will turn a corner.

Some Burning Epiphany

When road to return back home was far from sight
And the journey through life took a long and wayward turn,
Along a lost highway in the dark and heavy rainfall,
Then some burning epiphany took hold of the soul,
A yearning apotheosis from outside of the storm,
Celestial grace was then not so hard to find,
Senses became heightened, more enlightened,
A state of peace became a state of mind,
No longer lost and distracted but standing in the light,
A burdensome cloud lifted and the route was clear,
Out of the hurricane, to calm shoreline and sea,
Some burning epiphany took hold of my soul.

Sometimes, in an altered state
You can't find the way home,
Or move on to discover a finer place,
On dark byways, on a lost highway,
The reason why becomes an empty space.
Sometimes, all that's needed is a place to be,
To keep the faith, not just washed out
In some faded scenery, on a freeway,
On a stairway to a better understanding
Of the rightful destiny.

Some burning epiphany took hold of my soul,
Left me standing in clearer light,
Took the fragments and made them whole,
When the dark road back home was far from sight
Some burning epiphany restored the purpose in me.

Many and Varied Shades of Blue

Deeply immersed in a cool, deep hue,
Radiant ocean, Mediterranean horizon
In many and varied shades of blue,
Morning glory right there in view,
Out of this magic, into slow motion
Dreams tumbling through a skyline true,
Forgiven, forbidden, lost and hidden
Where calmness meets commotion,
Silence fades and a reckoning is due
In many and varied shades of blue.

Steeply versed on some cool avenue,
Eminent notion, subterranean devotion
In many and varied shades of blue,
Dawning story right there in view,
Into this moment, out of creation
Words falling through like morning dew,
Embraced, forsaken, found and taken
Where kindness greets with fascination,
Silence comes and is beckoning us too
In many and varied shades of blue.

Deep, cool hue in many and varied shades of blue.

Winter Days In To Reborn Spring Will Slip

Subtle tones and shades of advancing spring,
Open a mind to fresh imagining,
Fill the senses, entice our vision,
A moment to ponder and please the eye,
Crocus and snowdrop break through to blue sky,
Random leaves in spiral air currents caught,
Life on fast forward, precious time short,
Passes by, within an ephemeral thought.

Snowflakes fall between wild and naked trees,
Stir woodland not yet free from winter's grip,
Stop for one moment, just pause for a while,
Let nature's sweet and gracious gifts beguile,
Winter days in to reborn spring will slip
When a still and observant spirit sees,
Catch your reflection at the water's edge
Where herons glide across a silver lake,
To enter this instant for heaven's sake,
To break the mirror and Winter Queen's pledge.

Fleet of foot, a slender heron takes wing
Out into bright day from a long night's passing,
Soon, sprightly, as the lively heron steps
Into the air, beyond lustrous surface,
A blend of pure elegance and hubris
Climbs in free flight and then gently ascends,
So new born spring begins as winter ends,
Cold darkness to a warmer light transcends.
Now here is the evident thing, methinks
The lady doth love the spring.

We Two, This is Us

With you I collaborate,
Co-operate, my soul mate,
Together we both plan,
Resonate and ruminate,
Traverse the Earth's span
Together in this earthly state
We do the best we can,
Measure and navigate
Through stardust and the hands of fate.

Low roads and high roads,
Rivers, seas and lakes,
We are on this journey
For as long as it takes,
Through cloud bursts,
When the sun breaks
Through fair or heavy weather,
We are on this journey
Where love binds us together.

With you I may transcend,
Comprehend, my best friend,
Together we both stand,
Time we treasure and spend,
Reason and comprehend
Together in this firmament
We complement and blend
Like promise within a parable,
Happiness is blessed
In a chemistry incomparable.

With you I celebrate,
Deliberate, my soul mate,
Together we both scan,
Recognise and appreciate,
A woman and a man
Together in this earthly state
We do the best we can,
Measure and navigate
Through stardust and the hands of fate.

FROM THE ELUSIVE MUSE'S LEXICON

This is who we are,
This is what we do
With the minimum of fuss
Together we are true
We two, this is us!

Along Cathiron Lane, New Year's Eve 2017

Tony and Jane along a leafy Cathiron Lane,
An image brought to mind by a Cymbeline refrain,
Shake-spearean plots echo among forget me nots,
Amid rhymes, school bells chime to beckon dunces and swats,
But the cycle of the seasons with the mind does play a game
As it re defines borderlines across merit and blame,
It was nineteen-sixty-nine now its twenty-seventeen
And I'm sketching in spaces of the moments in between,
A carousel of faces pass like raindrops through the light,
Recollection races, leaves fine traces across this night,
Strange imagining or evidence, which am I to believe?
Bells, firecrackers break the pensive silence of New Year's Eve.

So the mordant, the discordant being banished from this day
When recall of the record in blinding foreground holds sway,
Where a river in timeless tarry through the valley rolls on,
There the past and the present they do merge and meet as one,
What of this journal, this infernal spirit here springing forth,
If the World still falls in turmoil to the south and to the north?
Patterns of poison spread in rivulets of purest rain,
We regulate reason with antidotes to numb the pain,
Where everything has changed but it all remains the same
While dirty broadsheets find some new victim to defame,
Is there no place we can discover that is still serene?
All the highs and lows level up to the average and mean,
The impetus of conference it slowly blows away,
Significance dissipates, is there nothing left to say?
I rescue my heart from where it sits upon my sleeve,
Revellers are rollicking and rolling on New Year's Eve.

Tree of Gold and Universal Dust

To see through winds and sands of time,
Blown salt sea strands, old hands of grime,
To where figures all breathed new life for me
In withered branches of a family tree.

And was this tree aflame with fire,
Did it extinguish hopes
Or burn with desire?
Twisted branches of gold dust and grime,
Entangled free souls
In their fall and climb,
Gave light to their own rise and shine
On an earnest and most jocular journey
Down passageways of former times,
To complete an unchartered itinerary
Along corridors they once defined,
A depleted and valiant tapestry
Where they walked an unbroken line.

Back in the annals of universal dust,
Along DNA strands between gold and rust,
To see through winds and sands of time,
Blown salt sea strands, old hands of grime.
A tree of gold and universal dust
Of happenstance and heresy,
Gave shape to a descendancy.

From Whence Came the First Origins of Man

From whence came the first origins of man,
A human presence, footsteps abroad
In the prescient, promised land,
When creation first stirred and life began?
First traces of the human DNA strand
Link Eden to Ethiopia,
Deep in the heart of Africa,
A garden in Somalia.
Somewhere in this heartland
Origins of the species were born,
Fused with colossal form,
Through the gateway
To this world we ventured,
The evolution seed passed down,
Mixed in the elemental age of existence
As languages and creeds were sown,
Flesh and blood and stars made known,
Souls anchored and dream scape mapped,
Fundamental concepts wrapped in destiny
Then thrown into seas of fire and wind,
Grains of sand and landscapes of holy resolution
Made solid in the light of immortal Heaven
Of time, and speed and physical space and calm and chemical chaos...

Creation versus evolution; the hands of divine omnipotence
Versus a scientific solution for the origins of human existence?
So, our life on Earth is down to one, magnificent, happy accident
Or the divine intervention of a supreme being, an indeterminate entity.
Excuse me while I drift on the threshold of infinity for a short interlude
To contemplate the inevitable question, whichever way you approach it,
Where did it all go wrong?

Meanwhile Celestial Pie in the Sky is next on the Menu...

A Slice of Celestial Pie

While you're chasing a piece of that pie,
Life may be passing right through,
Life may be passing on by,
Life may be slipping away from you
While your dreams they wither and die.
Well freedom may wake us up,
Pour of its vital nectar
There into an empty cup,
Fix the mind's eye toward a dream,
A conscious odyssey, to break the spell,
Kill all safe routine.
And if freedom is just a word
Then let's search for definition,
First it has to be heard
To gain some recognition,
Then it has to be taken,
No time to delay the decision
For freedom is so often forsaken.
While you're racing under that sky,
Life may be passing right through,
Life may be sailing on by,
Life may be stealing its light from you
While your dreams disappear in a sigh.
Take that piece of celestial pie,
Eat that slice and don't think twice,
Kick mud into convention's eye,
Break that slice of celestial pie,
The Gods are smiling down on you
As they amuse themselves on high.

For Absent Friends

Thinking of you here
In this quiet atmosphere,
Not really reminiscing
Just somehow missing you,
I cannot say why exactly
There is no explanation,
Suddenly you came to mind
Through some passing situation.
Hope all is well in your world
Any bad times getting better,
When I stop to think awhile
I suppose I should write you a letter.

Maybe I will never see you again,
Perhaps I'll see you tomorrow,
Look to me if there's someone you need
Or anything you wish to borrow,
I think of you from time to time
In odd moments I often recall,
As long as I am able to remember
I could not forget you at all.
For some unknown reason
I am thinking of you here,
Not really reminiscing
In this quiet atmosphere.

This One is for J.B.

Well Charlie Mingus once said,
"Better Git It In Your Soul",
Have to give it all you've got
If you're gonna let it roll,
So from Grantham Street to Camden Town,
Around the World and down the road,
Behind the drum kit, in the hot seat,
He was laying down that backbeat
While playing in the Two-Tone mode,
Underneath the spotlight, a la Bebop,
Hitting the rim shot, perfectly in time.

Back down along time's Green Avenues
During those halcyon dues of school,
Just a group of youthful confidantes
Checking out all the Gurus of cool,
Flush with youth and years ahead of us,
A direction in life yet to choose,
There was soul, Motown, Blue Beat and Ska
And a drum set to Break out the Blues,
Then listening in to all that Jazz
Before life's heavy Razzamatazz,
Parting ways when you follow that star.
The song lyric, "Black, White, Stop the Fight"
Way back in nineteen-sixty-eight,
After Martin Luther King's speech "I have a Dream!",
Profound words to which we could all relate.
Later, when the great man was still in jail
Before Apartheid became history,
Then it seemed a racist state couldn't fail,
The Band was playing set Mandela free!

So, when You're Wondering in some Ghost Town
Why this world can remain so strange,
Remember, music and unity hold power,
The power to deliver change,
As people sharing life's journey
In the search for what makes us whole,
They say the truth can set you free,
"Better Git It In Your Soul".
From Grantham Street to Camden Town,
Around the World and down the road,
Behind the drum kit, in the hot seat,
He was laying down that backbeat
While playing in the Two-Tone mode,
Underneath the spotlight, a la Bebop,
Hitting the rim shot, perfectly in time.
So whatever it is we choose to do
And if the truth can set us free,
In the search for what makes us whole
On the course of life's journey,
Then this one is for J.B.
Bless you Buddy,
He had natural rhythm,
Deep down in his soul.

When The Rules Get Burned (The Death of Democracy)

Sacred, factual texts of history trashed,
Human values, tenets, through centuries learned,
Tarnished leaders they parade unabashed,
Principles, law, correct practice overturned,
Pure truth is spurned when the rules get burned.

All results were fixed, the future has no past,
Rigged without involvement of those concerned,
Tainted speakers give tirades in their bombast,
Ignore votes passed and void the ballots returned,
Belief is scorned when the rules get burned.

Voices are silenced as more darkness descends,
To create deception no stone is left unturned,
Stealth in advancement, the disappearance of friends
By identities that will not be discerned,
The tide has turned when the rules get burned.

Rationale abandoned, reason distorted,
False honours awarded without being earned,
Air frequencies loaded and pure logic thwarted,
Justice on vacation, fairness adjourned,
Faith becomes torn up when the rules get burned.

Networks erected that favour the ignoble
Where the worst of fears they all get confirmed,
Corruption's scale of proportions global,
An answer is always that "lessons are learned",
Hope is made forlorn when the rules get burned.

Words and soundbites hide a lack of sincerity,
The vulnerable by austerity churned,
Those without need grow personal prosperity,
Rightful change is hard won, even surely yearned,
We all stand warned when the rules get burned.

At the News of a Death

Must it end right here
So quiet and common,
On this dog awful day
Of dark deed solemn?
From the man-made maze
Of three-dimensional dust,
Where children green gaze
Upon killers of our trust,
For it leaves one cold
This departure so swift,
As storm clouds gather
At the loss of his gift.
Though almost miniscule
In its measure to me,
There were others for whom
It was as vast as the sea.
Will it fail to penetrate
My raised barrier shell?
Am I insensitive
To the toll of Death's bell?
Preached words ring on
As we take our next breath,
Then try to come to terms
With the news of a death.

One Wish for a Winsome Child

By cherubic mouth,
Sweet angel expression,
My breath it is taken away.
By whimsical wonder,
By innocence under a smile
That exudes from those wide eyes,
With one move you disarm me
The power to charm being there
In your innermost infant soul.
What pleasures you bring,
What joys should I sing,
To celebrate how you elevate
The spirit and render me whole.
With eyes wide open
You give forth a token
Of tenderness to treasure eternal,
Beyond plans infernal
And promises broken
In love and life,
I make you this one wish;
No matter what ails you
Your spirit will sail through,
May your welfare be charmed
And as deeply felt as my bliss.

Something for Posterity

Something for posterity
Remembered in lost time,
To wash vainglorious over me
In a broken paradigm,
A moon dog wail of heresy
Somewhere down the line,
Marks an absence of courtesy
But the tone is anodyne.
A spark of bright intensity
Its fine embers fire the mind,
To win victorious over me
Awoken and benign,
A lark of promiscuity
For the page to find
Something for posterity
But the mood is philistine.
When opaque turns to clarity
Then the slender clock does chime,
To strike censorious over me
And castigate lost time,
Youth, beauty, physicality,
Somewhere down the line
Make way for age and gravity
For the hours are serpentine,
So something for posterity here
To decipher in your own time.

What's in a Title?

*An Exclusive Cruise to Babylon……
*Some Intrusive Blues in Mexican…..
*Inclusive News from a Hexagon……
*Obtrusive Views of the Pentagon…...
*Abusive Clues in a Cryptogram…….
*Instructive Slews for a Histogram…..
*An Inveterate Ruse to an Anagram…

Or even…

"From the Elusive Muse's Lexicon"

A Second Volume of thoughts allowed…Reports out loud…
Poems, as a companion to the First Volume of Poetry…

"A Storm in Pandora's Tea Box"

From

Garry B Grove   July 2020

Dedications

Page 7: Poem, *"Sounds of the Rolling Sea"* - to my Grandson, Jamie Lewis Grove.

Page 16: Poem, *"Into the World of O'Carolan"* and

Page 18: Poem, *"Paean to a Departed Celtic Troubadour"* - to the late Mervyn Haran.

Page 30: Poem, *"Old Redwood Tree"* - to Kathy Prendiville and Clive Dixon.

Page 34: Poem, *"Green Avenues"* - to Pete Chambers, BEM.

Page 44: Poem, *"The Tenure of Childhood"* - to my Grandson, Thomas Elliot Grove

Page 52: Poem, *"Words of the Fisherman"* – to my brother, Arland C Grove.

Page 58: Poem, *"Winter Days In To Reborn Spring Will Slip"* and

Page 59: Poem, *"We Two, This Is Us"* - to Pauline and Julian Westwood.

Page 61: Poem, *"Along Cathiron Lane, New Year's Eve (2017)"* - to Jane and Tony French.

Page 66: Poem *"This One is For J.B."* – to John Bradbury 1953 - 2015.

And a very large thank you to my wife Isabelle, for being the slightly more accessible Muse, divine inspiration and saviour of my sorry soul.

www.ingramcontent.com/pod-product-compliance
Lightning Source LLC
Chambersburg PA
CBHW031417040426
42444CB00005B/610